POSITIVE PROSPECTS

CAREERS FOR SOCIAL SCIENCE GRADUATES AND WHY NUMBER AND DATA SKILLS MATTER

T0349476

The Campaign for Social Science was launched in 2011 to promote social science to the UK Government and the wider public.

We campaign for policies that support social science inquiry in the UK, such as the retention of large-scale longitudinal research programmes. We promote social science on social media and at events.

The Campaign is supported by a coalition of universities, learned societies, charities and publishers.

To contact the Campaign, please call: +44 (0) 207682 4663 or email: campaign@acss.org.uk

For further information on the Campaign, see:

www.campaignforsocialscience.org.uk

Twitter: @CfSocialScience

Facebook: www.facebook.com/CfSocialScience

The Campaign was launched and is sponsored by the Academy of Social Sciences, a company registered in England, number 3847936, and a registered charity, number 1088537.

POSITIVE PROSPECTS

CAREERS FOR SOCIAL SCIENCE GRADUATES AND WHY NUMBER AND DATA SKILLS MATTER

DR ASHLEY LENIHAN
SENIOR POLICY ADVISOR
CAMPAIGN FOR SOCIAL SCIENCE

AND

SHARON WITHERSPOON
HEAD OF POLICY
CAMPAIGN FOR SOCIAL SCIENCE

CAMPAIGN
for SOCIAL SCIENCE

Los Angeles | London | New Delhi
Singapore | Washington DC | Melbourne

CAMPAIGN
for SOCIAL SCIENCE

33 Finsbury Square
London
EC2A 1AG

Los Angeles | London | New Delhi
Singapore | Washington DC | Melbourne

SAGE Publications Ltd
1 Oliver's Yard
55 City Road
London EC1Y 1SP

SAGE Publications Inc.
2455 Teller Road
Thousand Oaks, California 91320

SAGE Publications India Pvt Ltd
B 1/I 1 Mohan Cooperative Industrial Area
Mathura Road
New Delhi 110 044

SAGE Publications Asia-Pacific Pte Ltd
3 Church Street
#10-04 Samsung Hub
Singapore 049483

Editor: Natalie Aguilera
Editorial assistant: Eve Williams
Production editor: Rachel Burrows
Copyeditor: Sarah Bury
Proofreader: Bryan Campbell
Marketing manager: Susheel Gokarakonda
Cover design: Lisa Harper
Typeset by: C&M Digitals (P) Ltd, Chennai, India
Printed in the UK

British Library Cataloguing in Publication data

A catalogue record for this book is available from the
British Library

ISBN 978-1-5264-6121-6

At SAGE we take sustainability seriously. Most of our products are printed in the UK using responsibly sourced papers and
boards. When we print overseas we ensure sustainable papers are used as measured by the PREPS grading system.
We undertake an annual audit to monitor our sustainability.

CONTENTS

FOREWORD

The Campaign for Social Science was set up in 2011 by the Academy of Social Sciences, to inform public policy and engage in evidence-informed advocacy about the importance of the social sciences. The Academy has over 1,100 Fellows, eminent academics and practitioners in business, government and other walks of society. Forty-two learned societies are also members, so that the Academy represents over 90,000 social scientists working throughout the United Kingdom. The social scientists we represent range from those in traditional academic settings to many others working in government, the private sector and the third sector, all using their social science knowledge and skills in their work.

The Campaign takes forward work not only to represent the social sciences, but is also concerned to promote the long-term health and well-being of the social science disciplines themselves. One of the Campaign's long-standing aims is to promote social science education that will equip the next generation of researchers with number and data skills so that the social sciences can play their full part in the important issues facing the UK.

This report is a contribution to that discussion. It shows that social science undergraduates have good employment prospects, even in the short-term after university. The findings build on previous work by the Campaign, published in 2013 that used 2010 data. But *Positive Prospects* uses updated data to take a more detailed look at employment destinations and outcomes for a range of social science disciplines. It also pulls together evidence about earnings. While there is variation among disciplines, and this report only examines destinations immediately after graduation, it shows that undergraduates in the social sciences generally have good employment prospects.

However, *Positive Prospects* highlights another message too. If undergraduates have number and data skills – either acquired at schools or as part of their undergraduate studies – they are likely to have a wider range of choices and possibly to earn more. In other words, these skills add a dimension that is valued by employers. This is not, of course, to say that number and data skills are the only thing that matters, or that all social science undergraduates need the same level of such skills. But it does show that having these skills offers additional opportunities to those who have them. The Campaign for Social Science also believes that it is important for students from a wide range of disciplines to have these skills so that the full range of disciplinary perspectives can be brought to bear in important policy and public debates using social science evidence.

Another important message in this report is that social science training and skills are in demand – often because they provide the appropriate level of rigour, subject-specific knowledge, conceptual thinking and intellectual curiosity that meets the needs of a fast changing labour market. Social scientists currently in the education pipeline will be able to blend what they know and how they think with other disciplines. These intersections are increasingly the hallmark of a future knowledge economy that will rely on technical mastery alongside critical thinking.

This report was originally aimed at giving information useful to social science undergraduates and to school students considering studying social sciences in their undergraduate years. With the recent announcement of the Government's review of higher education, it will also undoubtedly be relevant to debates about employment prospects after university. The findings here will challenge presentations of an over-simplified picture of employment prospects by discipline, since the report gives some indication of just how many factors come into play, and how there is variation in STEM subjects as well as the social sciences.

The Campaign wishes to thank SAGE Publishing for their support and for publishing this report. We have also produced summaries for schools and school students, and for undergraduates. We will look forward to further discussion about the issues raised by the report with diverse audiences, including learned societies, universities, policy-makers and others.

Professor Shamit Saggar CBE FAcSS
Chair, Campaign for Social Science

ACKNOWLEDGEMENTS

The Campaign for Social Science would like to thank SAGE Publishing for their support in making this report possible.

We also thank the staff at the Higher Education Statistics Agency for their help in providing the data and for providing guidance about their use.

1

INTRODUCTION

Almost 4 out of 10 students graduate from university with a social science degree.[1]

What do we mean by the term '*social science*'? In this report we take a broad view, but at root the social sciences are disciplines linked by their common 'focus on the study of contemporary human societies, economies, organisations and cultures, and their development'.[2] Where possible in this report, we include information for a wide-range of social science fields including: *social studies* (like politics, economics, sociology, and geography); *business & administrative studies* (like finance and accounting); *architecture, building & planning* (like urban planning); *law*; *education*; and *psychology*.[3]

UK social science graduates have good employment prospects.

After their undergraduate degrees, they go on to work in a wide range of sectors and occupations, with employment rates similar to graduates in STEM (science, technology, engineering and maths). Social science graduates are valued not only for their discipline-specific knowledge, but also for their critical analysis and writing skills, which are especially important in many of the professional and management jobs for which they are hired.[4]

This report describes where UK social scientists go to work in their first jobs.

In part, it updates a previous Campaign for Social Science report on graduate destinations that looked at students who graduated in 2008/09.[5]

Here we focus on students who graduated in 2015/16. But this report also covers new topics. We look at how the prospects of graduates across the many disciplines of social science may vary, as well as at differences between male and female graduates. We include information about outcomes for those attending different types of university. Finally, we add coverage of student number and data skills, and what difference these skills may make to employment prospects. This includes a brief look at pathways from AS/A level to university and subsequent employment.

This report adds coverage of data and numbers skills because of their potential to increase the opportunities of social science graduates after university.

In many of today's jobs – and for virtually every major challenge faced by the UK – there is a need to bring together social scientists' general analytic skills and knowledge of society with better understanding and use of data of all sorts (ranging from 'big data' to surveys to individual data). Data have transformed the information available to decision-makers in public policy, healthcare, education, and the private sector. To ensure that social science insights can play their part, and to ensure continued buoyancy in the employment prospects of social science graduates, more social scientists need to engage with the growing need for number and data skills, alongside their existing ability to use all types of information to describe and analyse.

So this report aims to encourage a larger number of those interested in social science – whether school students preparing for university or undergraduates – to consider how they might better engage with number and data skills. In the UK, AS level mathematics intake is falling, which has been attributed to the decoupling of AS and A levels,[6] and many secondary school students have little exposure to using numbers and data to examine social science issues within their subjects. The evidence presented here shows why that matters.

This report proceeds as follows. Chapter 2 examines the career, employment, and earnings prospects of UK social science graduates, updating our 2013 report '*What do social science graduates do?*'. Chapter 3 looks at the future outlook for UK social scientists, highlighting the skills that will be needed in the future, especially in light of the digital revolution. Chapter 4 looks at pathways from school to university to employment, focusing in particular on the importance of number and data skills. Chapter 5 concludes the report with a discussion of some implications for higher education and research, employers, policy-makers and students.

A final note. The information presented in Chapter 2, using HESA data, covers all UK universities and graduates. In Chapters 3 and 4, we note where data do or do not include evidence from Scotland or Wales or Northern Ireland.

2

PROSPECTS

UK social science graduates have favourable employment prospects, with good earning potential throughout the course of their careers.

EMPLOYMENT RATES

When we look at the big picture – at the social sciences, the other sciences, and the arts and humanities[7] – the employment rates of graduates from UK universities do not differ significantly from one another a year after graduation (see *Figure 1*).

According to 2015/16 data from the Higher Education Statistics Agency (HESA), 66% of full-time, first-degree students in the social sciences were employed in the UK or abroad one year after they graduated, in comparison to 70% in the sciences and 66% in the arts & humanities. This means that at least two-thirds of each group were in full-time employment. If we include those who also combined their employment with further study, the number of those in work rises to almost three-quarters for each group (72% for the social sciences, 74% for the other sciences, and 72% for the arts & humanities). An additional 18% of social science graduates, and 17% of graduates from the other sciences and the arts & humanities, chose to pursue further study without working. Just 5% of social science and science graduates, and 6% of arts & humanities graduates, reported that they were unemployed.[8] And remember, this is employment only one year after graduation, when some students will be taking a break of one sort or another.

Figure 1   Destinations of Full-Time UK Graduates, 2015/16[9]

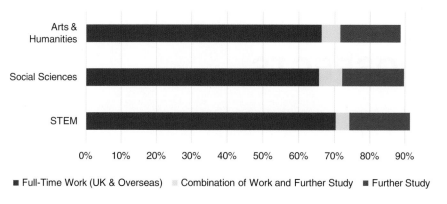

This means that about nine in ten (or 90%) of social science graduates are working, continuing their studies, or both, as are graduates from STEM (91%) or the arts & humanities (89%).[10]

Figure 2 provides an overview of the prospects for UK social science graduates across these different employment categories.

Employment rates do, of course, vary for those with different undergraduate degrees within this broader category of social science, just as they do for the different subjects within STEM or the arts & humanities (see *Figure 3*).

Figure 2   Destinations of Full-Time UK Social Science Graduates, 2015/16[11]

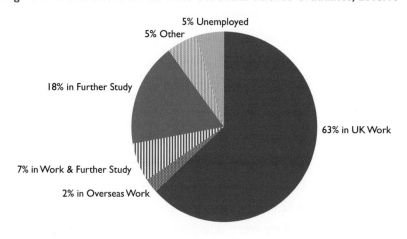

The gender gap in employment – the difference between the rates of male and female employment – also remains low, at 3% or below for most of the social sciences, and often favours female graduates (see *Figure 3*).

Figure 3 Percentage of Full-Time UK Graduates in UK and Overseas Work, 2015/16[12]

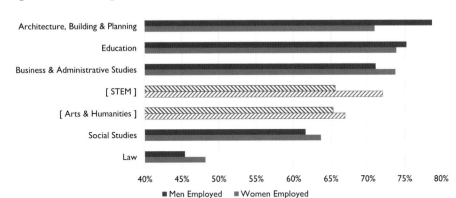

The employment rates of graduates with social science degrees improve with time. If we look at the data for the 2004/05 graduating cohort from the Department of Education's Longitudinal Education Outcomes (LEO) Dataset, for example, we see that although the number of those in sustained employment with or without further study varies by discipline, these numbers also rise over the five years after graduation for each discipline (see *Figure 4*).

Figure 4 UK Social Science Graduates in Sustained Employment with or without Further Study[13]

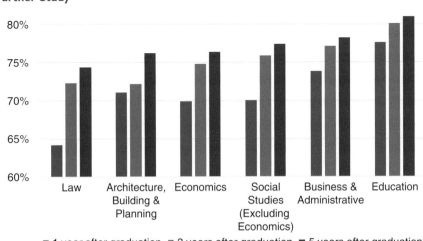

Of course, some social science subjects naturally have lower full-time employment rates right after graduation because these fields often require postgraduate study or training. If we include those in further study, or those who combine their studies with work, we see that there is a far larger percentage of graduates in these fields engaged in career-building activities. For example, 91% of UK law graduates are in work, further study, or both – as are 88% of graduates in social studies; 89% in business & administrative studies; and 94% in education (see *Figure 5*).

Figure 5   Destination of Full-Time UK Graduates, by Subject 2015/16[14]

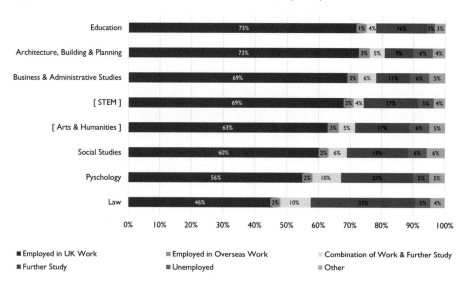

Looking at separate social science disciplines, prospects for employment are clearly related to whether students in different areas normally go on to postgraduate study. For example, as *Figure 6* shows, 81% of accountancy graduates will be in some form of work a year after graduation – as will 79% of architecture, 77% of finance, and 70% of economics graduates. Some professionalised degrees also have high employment right after graduation, like training teachers, of which 94% were in some form of work a year after graduation. Other professionalised degrees, as mentioned above, often require or encourage further study, like psychology where only 67% were in work a year after study, but another 23% were already in further study by that time.

Figure 6   Destination of Full-Time UK Social Science Graduates, by Principal Subject 2015/16[15]

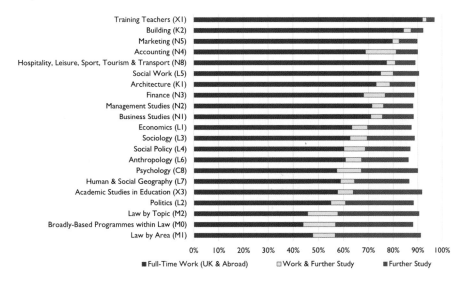

There also appear to be opportunities to improve these employment numbers for UK social science graduates, *if* they are able to demonstrate that they possess the types of number and data skills that employers of social scientists are increasingly looking for. This is explored further in Chapter 4.

SECTORS AND OCCUPATIONS

UK social science graduates go on to work in a wide range of sectors and occupations, confirming that their skills are useful in a range of fields.

Data from the HESA Destination of Leavers dataset for 2015/16 show that social science graduates leave university to work in a wide range of industries, from finance to public administration (see *Figure 7*). Looking across the social sciences as a whole, almost two in every ten graduates go into either the education or the professional, scientific, and technical activities sector. Other popular industries include the financial and insurance activities sector, wholesale and retail trade, human health and social work activities, and public administration and defence – with almost one in ten graduates going into each one of these industries, respectively.

Figure 7   Industry of Full-Time UK Social Science Graduates Entering Employment in the UK, 2015/16[16]

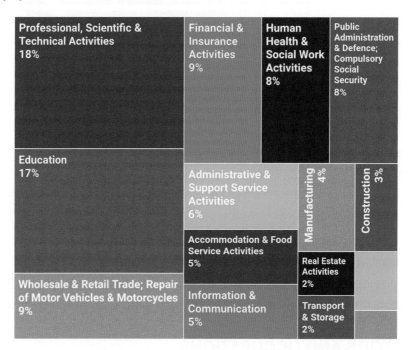

If we look at the separate degree subjects within social science, the pattern remains largely similar with some minor variations. *Figure 8* shows the top three choices of industry among full-time graduates entering employment for a selection of different social science degrees, ranging from psychology to finance.

Figure 8 Top 3 Industries of UK Graduates Entering Employment with a Selection of Specific Social Science Degrees, 2015/16[17]

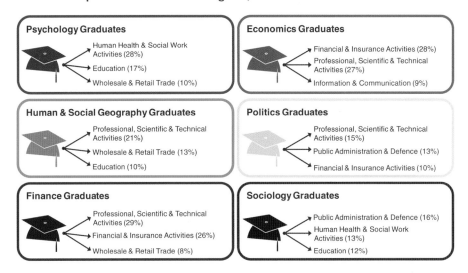

The HESA data also show that just over three-quarters (or 76%) of social science graduates leave university to work in some type of professional occupation as their first job (see *Figure 9*). The majority of the professional occupations that graduates enter are: business and public service associate professionals (31% of graduates); business, media and public service professionals (17% of graduates); and teaching and education professionals (11%).

Just under a quarter (or 24%) of social science graduates leave university to work in non-professional occupations. The most popular among these include administrative (8%), caring personal service (6%), and sales occupations (3%). But remember, these are the very first jobs taken up within a year of graduation, so they are not necessarily where graduates end up.

The number of social science graduates going into professional occupations does, however, vary by discipline. *Figure 10* shows the top three choices of occupation among full-time graduates entering employment for a selection of specific social science degrees. While 58% of psychology and sociology graduates enter 'professional' occupations, over three-quarters of geography (78%), politics (76%), and finance (78%) students do. In other fields, the numbers are far higher, with almost nine out of ten (or 89%) of economics graduates entering professional occupations. Again, in Chapter 4, we discuss whether some of these differences may relate to having number and data skills.

Figure 9 Occupation of Full-Time, First-Degree Leavers Entering Employment in the UK, by Subject Area of Degree 2015/16[18]

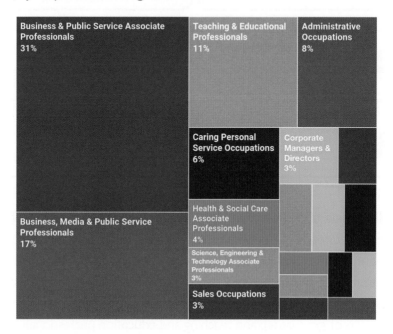

Figure 10 Top 3 Occupations of UK Graduates Entering Employment with a Selection of Specific Social Science Degrees, 2015/16[19]

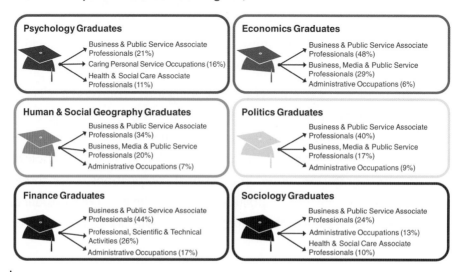

Many social scientists go on to be public leaders in the UK and abroad, demonstrating the valuable and wide-ranging skill-sets of these graduates.

A recent report from the British Council examined the educational and career pathways of over a thousand public and private sector leaders globally and found that 'most leaders have degrees in social sciences and humanities'.[20] That study found that 60% of global leaders are social scientists, with undergraduate degrees in education, business, or other social science fields (see *Figure 11*).[21]

In certain leadership roles, these numbers are even more stark: 61% of leading politicians internationally are graduates of the social sciences (including business and other social sciences).[22] Globally, social science graduates make up 62% of civil servant leaders, 70% of leading financial services and consulting professionals, and 93% of the leaders in law and legal services.[23]

There are also significant proportions of social science graduates in positions of leadership in fields that might not be expected. According to the British Council report, 50% of leaders in energy and environment, 46% of leaders in technology and innovation, 40% of leaders in health, and 35% of leaders in defence and security are graduates of the social sciences (including business and other social sciences).[24]

Figure 11   Undergraduate Subject Studied by Global Leaders[25]

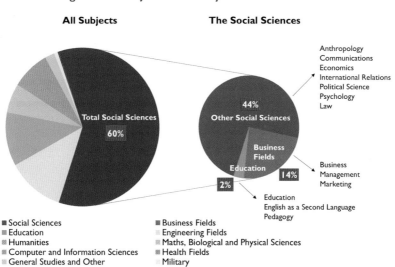

Moreover, more than half of these leaders held advanced (postgraduate) degrees in the social sciences and humanities, with a far larger proportion of these coming from the social sciences than from the humanities.[26]

EARNINGS

So far we have looked only at employment prospects for first jobs. We now look at what the data show about *earnings* after graduation. Individuals make their own choices about what subjects to study at school based on a wide range of factors – many of which are driven by what motivates and interests them – and earning levels are certainly not the only important aspect of work that determines the choices students make. But it is useful to know that the undergraduate subject choice may have an impact on future earnings potential.

Generally, social science graduates do well in terms of earnings. One year after graduation, the median salary of all UK-domiciled full-time graduates in the social sciences was broadly similar to the median salary of all subjects combined.[27] (All the earnings data presented in this report show earnings at the time, and have not been adjusted for inflation, so they would be higher in 2018/19.)

Figure 12   Median Salary of UK-Domiciled Full-Time UK Graduates, by Subject 2015/16[28]

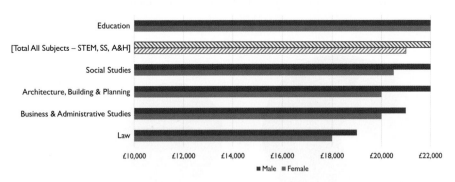

If we look at different subjects, economics graduates have a higher salary among the upper quartile of reported earnings one year after gradu-ation, than the graduates of other social science disciplines. The three social science degree subjects with the highest median salaries a year

CAMPAIGN *for* SOCIAL SCIENCE

after graduation are economics, building, and social work. We may expect that subjects with some of the highest salaries right out of university would include professionalised degrees where graduates may have less need to pursue further study to advance their careers in the near term, like building and social work.

But it is notable too that higher salaries are also associated with a number of subjects where we might expect students to graduate university with good number and data skills, like economics, finance, and business studies. *Figure 13* shows the lower quartile, upper quartile, and median salaries for social science graduates by principal subjects one year after leaving university, where there were at least 200 graduates surveyed. Economics students reported the highest earnings in the upper quartile, and some of the highest median and even lower quartile earnings, among graduates in the social sciences.

Figure 13   Salaries of Full-Time UK Social Science Graduates 2015/16, by Principal Subject[29]

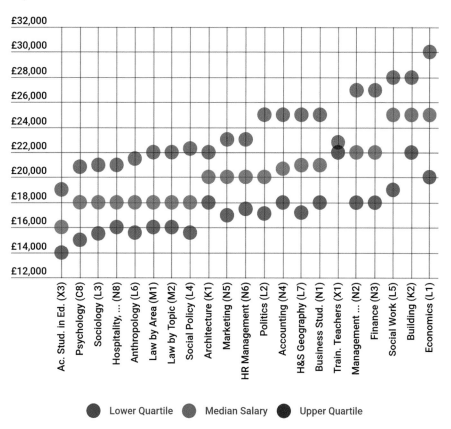

These are, of course, just the raw numbers. They do not control for other factors that will affect salary, and do not take account of the fact that different types of students choose different subjects. However, research conducted by Britton, Dearden, Shepard, and Vignoles in 2016 tells us that once different courses and student characteristics are taken into account, 'variation in graduate earnings are reduced', and for those graduates at the *lower* end of the earnings spectrum there is also 'little variation by subject' or gender.[30] Yet, within the group of graduates earning the *highest* salaries, 'subject matters more for both genders ... in particular graduates of medicine, law, economics, and languages continue to go on to achieve much higher earnings'.[31]

Britton *et al.* also found that both 'at the median and 90th percentile in most institutions [Law, Economics and Management] LEM graduates have higher earnings than graduates in STEM or in [other] subjects'.[32] This is probably due to the professional focus of these particular subjects. Interestingly, they also found that 'this effect is stronger at institutions that have higher median graduate earnings'. And they conclude that, 'within institutions, subject choice is important'.[33] So the subjects that undergraduates study and their institutions are both important for future earnings.

Figure 14   Median Earnings of UK-Domiciled First-Degree Graduates in 2003/04 from English Universities, Over Time and by Subject[34]

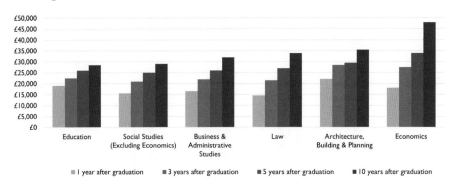

Looking at the most recently available data, social scientists also appear to do well over the life of their careers in terms of likely salaries. Data from the UK government's Department for Education Longitudinal Education Outcomes (LEO) Dataset for UK-domiciled first-degree graduates from higher education institutions (HEIs) in England show that social science graduates in all broad subject categories have good earnings growth potential over the course of their careers (see *Figure 14*).

For example, the median salary of a social studies graduates in 2003/04 – which includes graduates from politics, sociology, social policy, social work, anthropology, human and social geography, development studies, as well as those in other or broadly-based social studies programmes – rose from a median of £15,500 one year after graduation to £29,000 ten years after graduation.[35] Over that same period, income for graduates in education progressed from £19,000 to £28,500; in business and administrative studies from £16,500 to £32,000; in law from £14,500 to £34,000; and in architecture, building, and planning from £22,000 to £35,500.[36]

Subject choice matters to future earnings potential. In 2003/04, graduates in economics had a median salary of £18,000 one year after graduation, but this rose to £48,000 ten years later. This may be because economics graduates tend to have the type of number and data skills that make them attractive to employers, in addition to subject knowledge and access to employment opportunities in areas like financial services. As will be explored in Chapter 3, adding number and data skills to a student's personal 'skills toolkit' at AS/A level may increase the future options and earnings potential of undergraduates in other social science subjects as well.

INSTITUTIONS MATTER TOO

To place all of this in context, the university students attend can also influence future earnings.[37] If we start by looking at just the raw numbers, without controlling for other factors, graduates with degrees in the social sciences from Russell Group[38] universities tend to do better not just in terms of median salaries, but also in terms of the upper and lower quartiles of salaries they reported (see *Figure 15*). In 2015/16, for example, the highest earning economics graduates from a Russell Group university earned £32,500 one year after university versus those from non-Russell Group universities earning £28,000. The median reported salaries of Russell Group economics graduates were £4,400 more than their non-Russell Group counterparts, while reported salaries in the lower quartile were £2,500 higher than economics graduates from non-Russell Group universities. (Of course, part of this difference arises because students attending different universities may have different characteristics.)

Figure 15   Salaries of Full-Time UK Social Science Graduates in the UK, 2015/16, by Principal Subject[39]

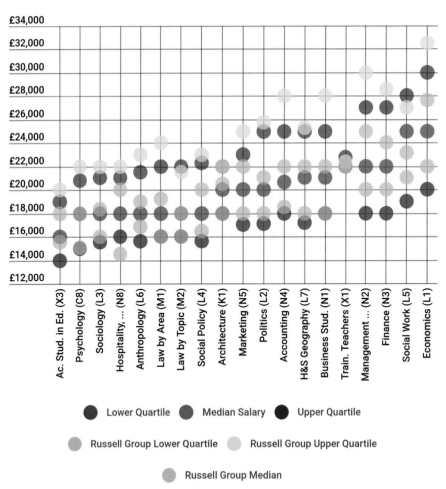

The research of Britton et al. shows that graduates of many of the UK's Russell Group universities are more likely to be in the top third of median annual earnings.[40] These differences are greater for males than females. London-based universities also generally do well in terms of graduate earnings, suggesting regional differences in where graduates go on to work (see *Figures 16* and *17*).[41]

Figure 16   Britton et al.'s Analysis of Female Median Earnings by Higher Education Provider (Reproduced with permission)[42]

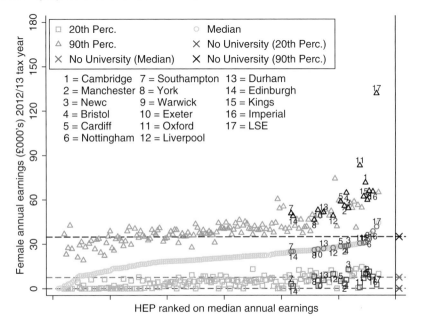

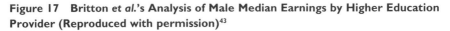

Figure 17   Britton et al.'s Analysis of Male Median Earnings by Higher Education Provider (Reproduced with permission)[43]

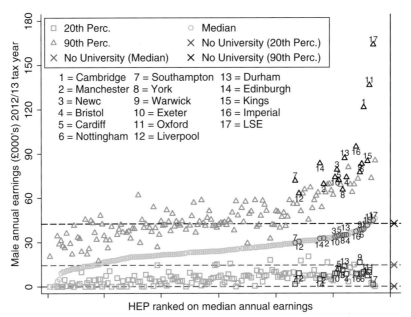

HEP ranked on median annual earnings

Britton et al.'s work also demonstrates that for both males and females there is 'strong evidence' that 'institution choice … conditional on subject choices' does matter. Their work shows that 'LEM earnings are much greater for some institutions than others' and that 'at the top end of the earnings distribution, institution choice matters more'.[44]

It should be noted, however, that the high reported earnings of graduates from some institutions may be due to the selectivity of these universities' entrance requirements. For example, when Britton et al. modelled predicted earnings at different UK universities to control for a number of factors, including previous academic attainment, they found that differences remained across institutions but that they were less dramatic.[45]

3
FUTURES

Social science graduates have a broad array of analytical skills that make them valuable to employers in the UK and abroad. But as the nature of work changes, especially in the context of the digital revolution, social scientists are likely to need to enhance their number and data skills – not only to ensure that they are able to successfully compete in tomorrow's job market, but also to ensure that they are able to play their part in solving the challenges that face society today.

In addition to their discipline-specific skill-sets, a recent report by the British Academy (*The Right Skills*) found that UK social science graduates possess a general set of skills (or 'core skills') that employers find valuable. These include the ability to communicate clearly and work effectively with others, their capabilities in designing research, collecting and analysing evidence, and making decisions, as well as useful behavioural and non-cognitive skills in problem solving, independence, creativity, and adaptability.[46]

But the workplace is changing, and many jobs now require number and data skills that may not have been as important in the past.[47] Research undertaken by Mason, Nathan, and Rosso in 2015 for the British Academy found that:

the growth in demand for QS [quantitative skills] reflects the impact of increasing pressures to improve efficiency and quality standards and engage in innovation, all of which require constant monitoring and interpretation of data of different kinds. At the same time, the widespread use of Information Technology (IT) in workplaces has not reduced the need for [quantitative skills] but rather changed the nature of the skills required.[48]

There are also new opportunities for those graduates with the ability to analyse, research, and track data, which are increasingly available on almost every aspect of our lives. These *big data*, collected from a range of everyday activities, are a vital and growing sector in the UK economy. A 2016 report from the Centre for Economics & Business Research (CEBR) estimates that 'from 2015 to 2020 ... the total benefit to the UK economy of big data analytics [will] amount to £241 billion, or £40 billion on average per year'.[49] Put another way, by 2020 the CEBR estimates that 'the value of big data analytics is expected to reach ... 2.2% of GDP'.[50]

As a result, social scientists with good number and data skills are needed in the UK economy now more than ever. Understanding the growing wealth of data available and being able to use it to help solve the challenges we face globally and nationally – from the environment to disease control – will benefit from a social science understanding of society, human behaviour and interaction. Number and data skills 'are rarely used in isolation and often need to be combined with other generic skills',[51] such as social science understanding, to be most effective.

For example, there is a growing need for social scientists who can use data to improve health-related behaviour, to help with urban and rural planning, to assess 'what works' in education, and so on.[52] It is important that these issues are considered by a wide range of disciplines, including geographers and psychologists, sociologists and political scientists, and anthropologists as well as economists and lawyers – and number and data skills will be important if each discipline is to play its part.

Moreover, those in the technology sector are increasingly aware of the need for social scientists to help solve some of the unique social problems and challenges presented by advances in information and data technology.[53] This might mean helping to understand how new technologies like artificial intelligence might be accepted by society in different areas of our life, or providing guidelines for the ethical use of platforms like Facebook or YouTube. Already, companies like Google are helping to fund organisations like Full Fact to try to create an automated fact-checking system to help combat the growing issue of 'fake news'.[54] Or, as Hartley highlights in his recent book *The Fuzzy and the Techie*, it might mean a company developing driverless cars like Nissan hiring an anthropologist to 'design and lead company research into human machine interaction'.[55] As Hartley's work explains, 'though gaining literacy in tech tools is important' in order to contribute to innovation in the tech sector, 'a technical degree is not required'.[56]

There is a high demand for number and data skills in the UK labour market, across graduates from all disciplines.[57] In their research, Mason *et al.* found that in looking at the 'highest level of quantitative skills used in jobs' among 20 to 60 year-olds, an increasing percentage felt that advanced mathematical and statistical skills were important to their work (see *Figure 18*). Looking at National Institute of Economic and Social Research (NIESR) estimates derived from the 2012 Skills and Employment Survey, they also found that advanced mathematical and statistical skills are 'essential or very important' for managers and professionals,[58] and that those professionals 'making essential or very important use of advanced QS mathematics/statistics are most commonly found' within those sectors that social scientists often populate, like 'financial services … business services … [and] education'.[59]

Figure 18   Importance of Advanced Mathematics and Statistics[60]

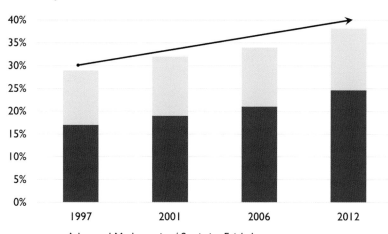

■ Advanced Mathematics / Statistics Fairly Important
■ Advanced Mathematics / Statistics Essential or Very Important

But while there is clearly a high demand for these skills in the UK labour market, there may not be enough people with number and data skills to meet demand in the future.[61] The early specialisation of UK secondary and higher education means that many social scientists entering the labour market now may not have taken any mathematics or statistics since they turned 16 – making it difficult for them to make the most of the many opportunities for interesting careers that are open to them today.

In a 2010 survey of 24 countries, Hodgen *et al.* (2010) found that only in England, Wales, and Northern Ireland do fewer than 20% of 16 to 19 year-olds study maths. The 2017 CBI/Pearson Education and Skills Survey found that 39% of UK school leavers did not achieve a GSCE Maths grade of C or better,[62] and 29% of UK employers are dissatisfied with school and college leavers' basic numeracy skills.[63] In 2016 the CBI/Pearson Survey found that the level of UK businesses that are 'not confident there will be enough people available in the future with the skills to fill their high-skilled jobs' had reached 69%.[64] Improving the number and data skills of social scientists entering the workforce may, therefore, do a lot to increase their appeal to UK employers.

4

PATHWAYS

The path from school to university to employment differs for everyone. The path students and undergraduates choose as social scientists will affect their personal 'toolkit' of skills. Having number and data skills as part of this 'skills toolkit' may not only increase future employment options, it may also help lead to higher earnings down the road.

AS/A LEVEL MATHS

The numbers of social science undergraduates who have completed AS or A levels in mathematics varies by the subject of their degree, partly because some disciplines require or encourage applicants to have them. But even those aiming to apply for other social science disciplines might benefit from pursuing a qualification that improves their number and data skills.

Figure 19 shows the proportion of undergraduates going into university with either an AS, A, or IB in mathematics, using data from the 2017 Interim Report on the *Mathematical Backgrounds of Undergraduates* by Hodgen *et al.* That report groups the broader degree fields by how mathematically 'demanding' they are – according to whether entering students have a high, medium, or low level of number skills when studying them.[65] Hodgen *et al.* argue there tends to be a medium level of background in number skills among most of the

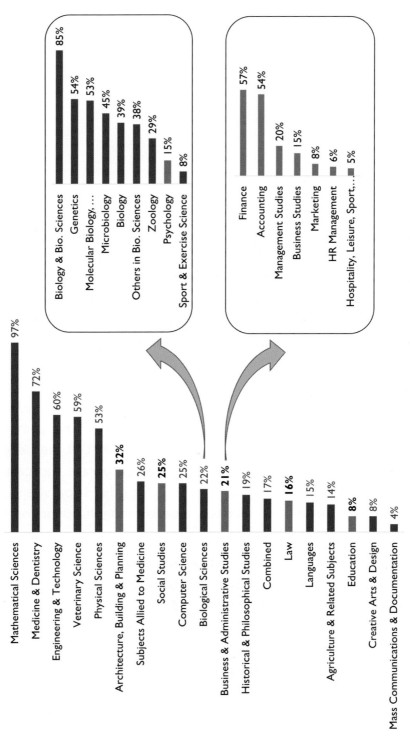

Figure 19 Mathematical Backgrounds of Undergraduates[66]

Mathematical Sciences — 97%
Medicine & Dentistry — 72%
Engineering & Technology — 60%
Veterinary Science — 59%
Physical Sciences — 53%
Architecture, Building & Planning — **32%**
Subjects Allied to Medicine — 26%
Social Studies — **25%**
Computer Science — 25%
Biological Sciences — 22%
Business & Administrative Studies — **21%**
Historical & Philosophical Studies — 19%
Combined — 17%
Law — **16%**
Languages — 15%
Agriculture & Related Subjects — 14%
Education — **8%**
Creative Arts & Design — 8%
Mass Communications & Documentation — 4%

Biology & Bio. Sciences — 85%
Genetics — 54%
Molecular Biology,… — 53%
Microbiology — 45%
Biology — 39%
Others in Bio. Sciences — 38%
Zoology — 29%
Psychology — 15%
Sport & Exercise Science — 8%

Finance — 57%
Accounting — 54%
Management Studies — 20%
Business Studies — 15%
Marketing — 8%
HR Management — 6%
Hospitality, Leisure, Sport,… — 5%

■ Social Science Subjects ■ All Other Subjects

broader social science subject groupings, with the exception of law, where a relatively low level of number skills is common (though students might benefit if they have them). But even *within* the broad subject groupings, there is much variation depending on the specific subject being studied, as the extracts for biology and business studies show.

For example, across the broader field of 'business and administrative studies' as a whole, only about two out every ten students entered university with a post-16 maths qualification. Yet, in fact, more than five out of ten incoming university students doing degrees in finance or accounting were reported to have a post-16 maths qualification, while fewer than one in ten of students doing degrees in marketing or human resources management had such a qualification.

Another report (by Hillman 2014) gives more detailed data about the mathematics qualifications of those entering social sciences at university in 2007 and 2010. As *Figure 20* shows, only in economics do as many as six out of ten entrants to university have A level mathematics. For geography and psychology, the figure was around two out of ten entrants, while fewer than one in ten or one in twenty of those studying political science or sociology (respectively) did so.

This matters for various reasons. First, it limits the types of questions and evidence that different social science disciplines can look at. And second, it means that graduates from these disciplines are less likely to have the number and data skills that employers increasingly seek.

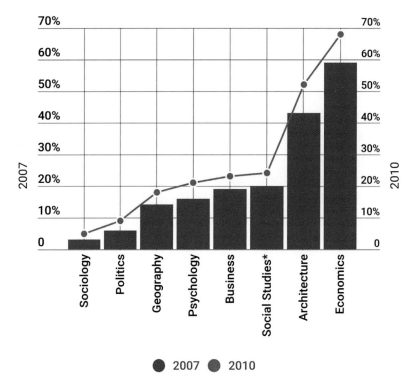

● 2007 ● 2010

Before reforms to the UK curriculum put in place in 2016, the numbers of students taking A level mathematics was growing steadily, but the numbers of students taking AS level was growing at an even higher rate (see *Figure 21*). Changes since then, however, have meant that AS level mathematics is no longer encouraged as a stand-alone qualification and there is no longer funding to promote its uptake by students. Figures from the Joint Council for Qualifications show that fewer students took AS level mathematics in 2016 and 2017 than did so in 2015, and the numbers of those pursuing the qualification seem to be on a downward trajectory (see *Figure 21*).

Figure 21 AS and A Level Mathematics Entries (UK)[68]

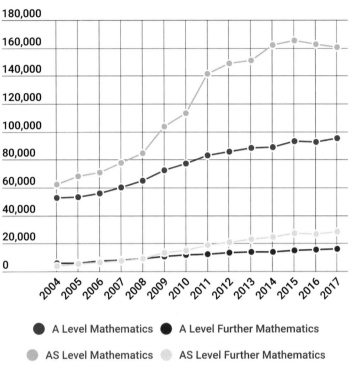

This is a concern, since for many going on to study the social sciences, AS level mathematics or statistics are an important way of refreshing and increasing number and data skills, especially given the increasing focus on statistics in both academic and professional settings. Recent changes to school funding that encourage the uptake of A level mathematics may help to correct this problem,[69] but a stand-alone AS level qualification in mathematics still has value for those who want to pursue a degree or a career in the social sciences, but who may not wish to take a full A level in mathematics.

IMPACT OF NUMBER AND DATA SKILLS ON EARNINGS

We have previously noted that having number and data skills may open up more choices for students studying social sciences, and that the 'grand challenges' facing the UK would benefit if more people had both number and data skills and social science training. But there is evidence too that taking A level mathematics or statistics has a positive impact on earnings after graduation, regardless of what subjects are studied at university. Research by Adkins and Noyes (2017) found 'compelling evidence of continued wage returns up to 11%' for those who have taken A level mathematics,[70] and 'a potential 7–10% increase in earnings by age 33' for those who have taken A level mathematics or computing.[71] It also seems reasonable to think that AS level mathematics, even as a stand-alone qualification, may have an impact on future earnings. In any case, Adkins and Noyes, for example, also found that 'mathematical skills, whether measured as ability scores at age 10, qualification grades at age 16 or completion of A level Mathematics, have a strong and positive association with earnings at age 34'.[72]

Figure 22 Britton et al.'s Analysis of Female Annual Earnings by Subject (Reproduced with permission)[73]

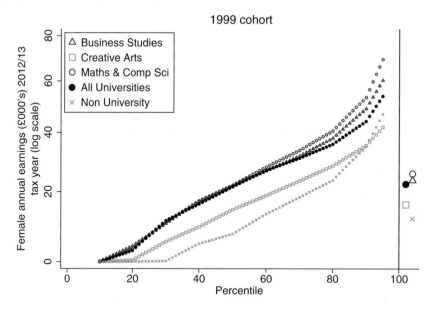

Figure 23   Britton et *al*.'s Analysis of Male Annual Earnings by Subject (Reproduced with permission)[74]

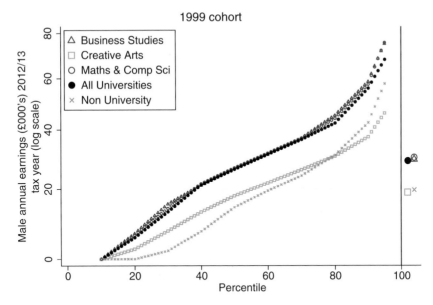

Of special interest to female students is the 'wage gap' of about 20% between the earnings of men and women in the UK by the age of 34.[75] Part of this is because of the different patterns of subjects men and women tend to take from age 16 on. Yet, according to Adkins and Noyes, although women are less likely to take A level mathematics than men,[76] those women who *do* choose to take A level maths receive a *higher* wage return for doing so than their male counterparts.[77]

This suggests that having good number and data skills, in combination with the discipline-specific and 'core' social science skills of analysis and communication, are likely to help students' long-term employment prospects.

If we group subjects by the level of number skills they demand,[78] it appears that graduates of subjects with a medium demand for quantitative skills – i.e. those which require some number and data as well as other skills – appear to have among the highest numbers in employment or further study one year after graduation, and that these numbers are generally higher for women (see *Figure 24*).

Figure 24   Percentage of Full-Time First-Degree Leavers in UK or Overseas Work, by the Level of Mathematical Demand Required by their Degree Subjects, 2015/16[79]

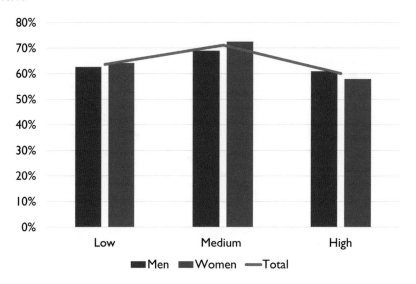

Graduates from social science subjects that are more likely to employ number and data skills, and who are more likely to have A level mathematics, also appear to do particularly well in terms of earnings. *Figure 25* uses data from an Index created by Sloane and O'Leary (2004), which shows the percentage returns to a variety of undergraduate degrees, controlling for student quality, in relation to an arts degree. A male graduate in accountancy, for example, was found by Sloane and O'Leary to have an hourly earnings premium of 42% relative to an arts graduate, and a female graduate in accountancy a premium of 37%.[80] This Index helps to highlight the higher earnings return for graduates from social sciences like accountancy and economics, where students will often have both post-16 mathematics qualifications as well as other more general skills in analysis.

Figure 25 Estimated Earning Returns to University Degrees by Subject[81]

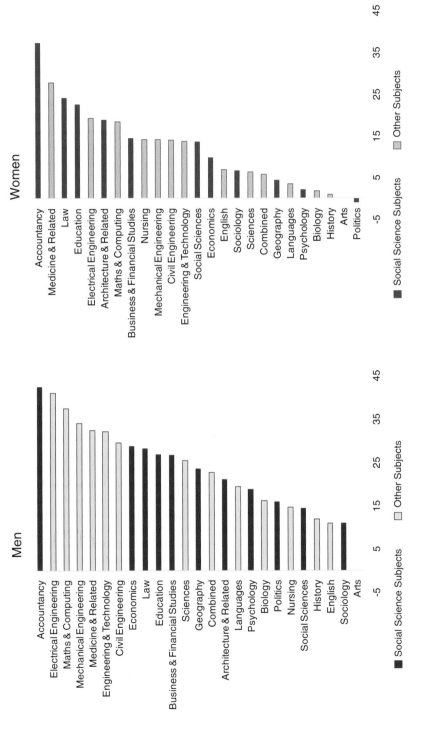

5

CONCLUDING THOUGHTS

The evidence in this report has come from many sources, looking at different graduating cohorts, and at data that did not follow particular individuals from 16 through to employment. This means that we have to be careful in making claims about causes; we are certainly not saying that taking A level maths in addition to, say, any particular social science degree will *definitely* mean getting a secure job with a higher salary than would otherwise be the case.

It is clearly important, too, that students are engaged with and interested in what they are studying, and that we recognise there are many different pathways and skills in the wide range of social science disciplines at university.

But taken together, the findings of the data we have analysed, the reports we have cited (and others from the United States, for example[82]) on the whole appear to tell a similar story. There is a compelling case to be made – to school students, undergraduates, universities and policy-makers – that the employment prospects of those studying undergraduate social sciences are good, and that having number and data skills may help give individuals more choices.

IMPLICATIONS AND RECOMMENDATIONS

For undergraduates

- Getting a good social science degree gives undergraduates skills that employers value. Social science undergraduates get a range of good jobs in a wide range of sectors and have good earnings prospects.

Some of these jobs will make overt use of your social science knowledge, but many others will depend on the skills in analysis, interpretation, writing and so on that social science helps impart.

- Different social science disciplines of course have different pathways and prospects. And the institution you attend matters, but along with other considerations – graduates from some universities earn more than others, but there are things you can do to increase your choices, whatever university you attend.

- Engaging with number and data skills during undergraduate study is likely to be helpful in giving you additional skills that are valued by employers, and can lead to interesting work and a wider range of career choices. Many universities are increasingly offering courses not just in 'methods' but on topics using data and number skills to look at interesting and important questions, where undergraduates can learn how to interrogate evidence in new ways. They may also help increase work opportunities and are likely to enhance future earnings potential. Whatever the discipline, it is worth considering engaging with courses that will improve your number and data skills.

For school students

- School students should consider A level choices carefully. Of course, grades do matter, but so too do the courses you choose to take. For the widest range of employment opportunities, students should consider what type of university they wish to attend. The more competitive the university, the more likely they are to seek 'enabling subjects', such as geography for aspiring social scientists, whatever discipline students intend to choose as their future degree field.

- School students should consider various ways in which they can continue to improve their number and data skills. For those who can and wish to, A level mathematics or statistics may be both useful for undergraduate studies and help in getting jobs afterwards. But A levels are not the only way to engage with number and data skills. Some schools still continue to offer AS level mathematics or statistics, and where that is an option it may be worth considering. Some schools offer 'Core

Maths', a variety of courses which continue to stretch thinking about numbers and data in a range of practical and academic areas. Some schools offer A level curricula in other social science subjects that use numbers and data within them. This could mean, for instance, considering taking A level social science courses that allow students to apply a range of number and data skills.

For schools

- The Campaign for Social Science will continue to work for policies that give the widest range of pathways to improve number and data skills for those who will study social science as undergraduates. Recent funding reforms for A levels may support schools to encourage more students to take A level maths.[83] But the Campaign for Social Science will continue to work for funding and support for AS mathematics and statistics at school, as an intermediate pathway for those who do not wish to take a full A level in maths.

- Engagement with 'Core Maths' is another possible option for schools. In addition, it is clear that some A level social science courses give wider options than others, and that different social science curricula from different examining bodies give varying degrees of experience[84] in using numbers and data. Future curriculum updates are likely to continue to raise expectations that A level students will learn how to use data, including numerical data, to examine issues. This is always challenging but is increasingly important in work.

For universities

- Students, including social science students, will increasingly benefit from gaining a range of number and data skills. This will matter for those who later seek postgraduate qualifications to become professional social scientists, but it is also likely to become increasingly important to employers. Many universities are already taking strategic decisions about this, for instance in the case of those that have 'Q-Step' centres. But all universities, and university social scientists, should be thinking about and discussing these issues. Of course, some students will not wish to gain these skills, but having a variety of appropriate expectations and pathways for students to acquire basic, intermediate or advanced number and data skills within the social sciences is something each university will need to consider in the light of its intake of students and where they go afterwards. A key message is that number and data skills should not be the sole concern of STEM disciplines or social science disciplines like economics.

For policy-makers

- Schools, universities, and employers need to work closely to send the signals and set incentives to make it possible for more students to continue taking post-16 mathematics and statistics in addition to their social science studies.
- The Campaign for Social Science supports the recommendations of the Smith Review[85] but would support their extension to a consideration of whether re-instating encouragement and funding for stand-alone AS level mathematics or statistics might be particularly useful for a large number of students. This is likely to include not only those students who aim to study social sciences or humanities at university, but even those in other disciplines (some biologists, for example).
- Core Maths should also be more widespread.
- If the UK is to make good its aspiration to improve the number and data skills of its future labour force, we need to move away from a 'zero-sum' approach of having only one pathway and instead offer multiple routes to gaining these skills.

APPENDIX: DETAILED MEDIAN EARNINGS

Figure 26 Median Earnings of Full-Time UK Graduates, 2015/16[86]

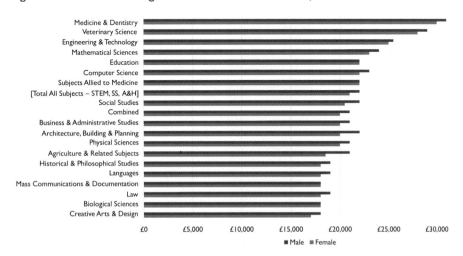

Medicine & Dentistry
Veterinary Science
Engineering & Technology
Mathematical Sciences
Education
Computer Science
Subjects Allied to Medicine
[Total All Subjects – STEM, SS, A&H]
Social Studies
Combined
Business & Administrative Studies
Architecture, Building & Planning
Physical Sciences
Agriculture & Related Subjects
Historical & Philosophical Studies
Languages
Mass Communications & Documentation
Law
Biological Sciences
Creative Arts & Design

£0   £5,000   £10,000   £15,000   £20,000   £25,000   £30,000

■ Male ■ Female

Figure 27 Median Earnings of Full-Time UK Social Science Graduates, 2015/16[87]

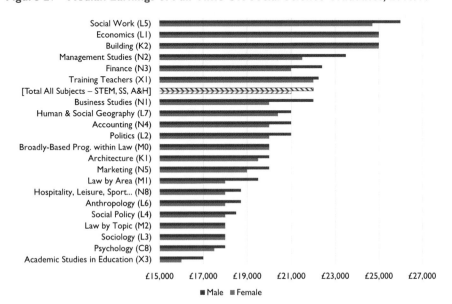

Social Work (L5)
Economics (L1)
Building (K2)
Management Studies (N2)
Finance (N3)
Training Teachers (X1)
[Total All Subjects – STEM, SS, A&H]
Business Studies (N1)
Human & Social Geography (L7)
Accounting (N4)
Politics (L2)
Broadly-Based Prog. within Law (M0)
Architecture (K1)
Marketing (N5)
Law by Area (M1)
Hospitality, Leisure, Sport... (N8)
Anthropology (L6)
Social Policy (L4)
Law by Topic (M2)
Sociology (L3)
Psychology (C8)
Academic Studies in Education (X3)

£15,000   £17,000   £19,000   £21,000   £23,000   £25,000   £27,000

■ Male ■ Female

Figure 28   Median Earnings of UK-Domiciled First-Degree Graduates in 2003/04 from English Universities, Over Time and by Subject[88]

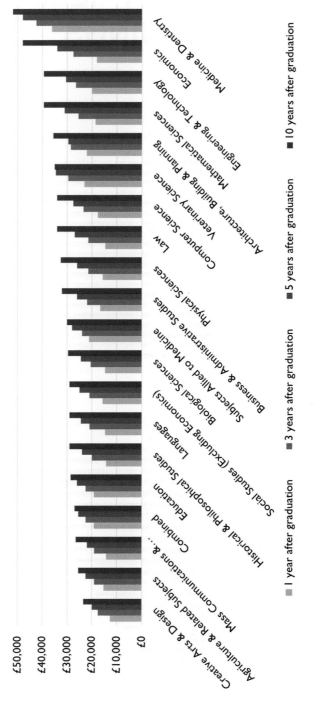

ENDNOTES

1   The proportion is 37%, which represents the proportion of full-time, first-time social science degree leavers from all UK HE providers and was calculated from principal subject data provided by HESA from the Destinations of Leavers Survey and Student Record 2015/16. Social Sciences total includes psychology (C8) graduates.

2   Bastow, S., Dunleavy, P. and Tinkler, J. (2014). *The Impact of the Social Sciences: How Academics and their Research Make a Difference*. London: Sage, p. 4. See pp. 3–6 for a more detailed discussion of their complete definition of 'social science', and what disciplines and fields may be considered to be 'social science'.

3   For the purposes of this report, we consider the social sciences to include the following broad subject areas from the Joint Academic Coding System (JACS) 3.0 classification system, in line with those included in Main Panel C covering social science for the Research Excellence Framework: Architecture, building & planning (JACS subject area code A, which includes principal subject codes K0, K1, K2, K3, K4, and K9); Social studies (JACS subject area code B, which includes principal subject codes L0, L1, L2, L3, L4, L5, L6, L7, L8, and L9); Law (JACS subject area code C, which includes principal subject codes M0, M1, M2, and M9); Business & administrative studies (JACS subject area code D, which includes principal subject codes N0, N1, N2, N3, N4, N5, N6, N7, N8, and N9); and Education (JACS subject area code I, which includes principal subject codes X0, X1, X2, X3, and X9). Wherever we had access to data at the more detailed 'principal subject' level, we have also included data on psychology graduates (JACS code principal subject code C8) within the total for social science. However, it should be noted that it was not always possible to do this, as HESA and JACS includes psychology graduates within their total figures for 'science' subjects, as it sits under the JACS subject area code 3 for the biological sciences. As a result, not all percentages/ tables in this report will be fully comparable between figures. But we have noted each instance throughout the report where psychology graduates could not be included within the totals for social science, allowing for comparison across figures where possible. Information on the JACS classification system used by HESA is available at: https://www.hesa.ac.uk/support/documentation/jacs/jacs3-principal.

4   'What do social science graduates do?', 2013, Campaign for Social Science, https:// campaignforsocialscience.org.uk/graduates-main/; Mason, G., Nathan, M. and Rosso, A. (2015). *State of the Nation: A Review of Evidence on the Supply and Demand of Quantitative Skills*. London: British Academy and NIESR.

5   'What do social science graduates do?', 2013, Campaign for Social Science, https:// campaignforsocialscience.org.uk/graduates-main/.

6   New AS and A levels in Mathematics and Further Mathematics were introduced in September 2017, but evidence from subjects decoupled earlier strongly indicate that AS level intake is falling in many subjects across the board, as a result of AS levels being decoupled from A levels. See: http://educationdatalab.org.uk/2016/08/a-level-results-day-2016-the-key-trends-in-four-charts/, and https://educationdatalab.org.uk/2017/08/a-level-results-day-2017-the-key-trends-in-three-charts/.

7   The 'other sciences' include the following subject areas from the JACS classification system, comprising both medicine and STEM (science, technology, engineering, and maths) subjects: (1) Medicine & dentistry; (2) Subjects allied to medicine; (3) Biological sciences; (4) Veterinary science; (5) Agriculture & related subjects; (6) Physical sciences; (7) Mathematical sciences; (8) Computer science; and (9) Engineering & technology. Again, where information was made available at a more detailed level, we have subtracted figures on psychology from the broader JACS category of the biological sciences. The arts & humanities include the following subject areas from the JACS classification system: (1) Mass communications & documentation; (2) Languages; (3) Historical & philosophical studies; and (4) Creative arts & design. Information on the JACS classification system used by HESA is available at: https://www.hesa.ac.uk/support/documentation/jacs/jacs3-principal.

8   Figures include UK and other EU-domiciled full-time, first-degree graduates from UK institutions, and were calculated from principal subject data provided by HESA from the Destinations of Leavers Survey and Student Record 2015/16. Proportions calculated based on the total of those in a known destination. Social Sciences total includes psychology (C8) graduates.

9   Figures include UK and other EU-domiciled full-time, first-degree graduates from UK institutions, and were calculated from principal subject data provided by HESA from the Destinations of Leavers Survey and Student Record 2015/16. Proportions calculated based on the total of those in a known destination. Social Sciences total includes psychology (C8) graduates.

10   Figures include UK and other EU-domiciled full-time, first-degree graduates from UK institutions, and were calculated from principal subject data provided by HESA from the Destinations of Leavers Survey and Student Record 2015/16. Proportions calculated based on the total of those in a known destination. Social Sciences total includes psychology (C8) graduates. It should be noted that only graduates in the veterinary, medical, or allied fields do significantly better on this measure. The percentage of graduates in employment or further study in medicine & dentistry is 99%, in subjects allied to medicine it is 96%, and in veterinary science it is 97%. Source: HESA Destination of Leavers from Higher Education in the United Kingdom for the Academic Year 2015/16, Table 6a – Destinations of full-time, first-degree leavers by sex, activity and subject area 2011/12 to 2015/16. Available at: https://www.hesa.ac.uk/news/29-06-2017/sfr245-destinations-of-leavers.

11 Figures include UK and other EU-domiciled full-time, first-degree graduates from UK institutions, and were calculated from principal subject data provided by HESA from the Destinations of Leavers Survey and Student Record 2015/16. Proportions calculated based on the total of those in a known destination. Social Sciences total includes psychology (C8) graduates.

12 Figures represent those in both UK and overseas work as a proportion of the total of those in a known destination. Please note that we did not have access to figures for psychology by gender, so psychology is not included here in the total figures for the social sciences, but is for STEM. Source: HESA Destination of Leavers from Higher Education in the United Kingdom for the Academic Year 2015/16, Table 6a – Destinations of full-time, first-degree leavers by sex, activity and subject area 2011/12 to 2015/16. Available at: https://www.hesa.ac.uk/news/29-06-2017/sfr245-destinations-of-leavers.

13 Figures represent all UK-domiciled first-degree graduates from English HEIs in the 2004/05 graduating cohort, and do not include psychology graduates. Data sourced from: Employment and Earnings Outcomes of Higher Education Graduates: Experimental Data from the Longitudinal Education Outcomes (LEO) Dataset, SFR60/2016, Table 1c, Department of Education.

14 Figures include UK and other EU-domiciled full-time, first-degree graduates from UK institutions, and were calculated from principal subject data provided by HESA from the Destinations of Leavers Survey and Student Record 2015/16. Proportions calculated based on the total of those in a known destination. Data for psychology (C8) graduates provided and are therefore subtracted from STEM totals.

15 Figures include UK and other EU-domiciled full-time, first-degree graduates from UK institutions, and were calculated from principal subject data provided by HESA from the Destinations of Leavers Survey and Student Record 2015/16. Proportions calculated based on the total of those in a known destination.

16 Figures include UK and other EU-domiciled full-time, first-degree graduates from UK institutions, and were calculated from principal subject data provided by HESA from the Destinations of Leavers Survey and Student Record 2015/16. Proportions calculated based on the total of all graduates surveyed (including those in an unknown destination). Social Sciences total includes psychology (C8) graduates.

17 Figures include UK and other EU-domiciled full-time, first-degree graduates from UK institutions, and were calculated from principal subject data provided by HESA from the Destinations of Leavers Survey and Student Record 2015/16. Proportions calculated based on the total of all graduates surveyed (including those in an unknown destination).

18 Figures include UK and other EU-domiciled full-time, first-degree graduates from UK institutions, and were calculated from principal subject data provided by HESA from the Destinations of Leavers Survey and Student Record 2015/16. Proportions calculated based on the total of all graduates surveyed (including those in an unknown destination). Social Sciences total includes psychology (C8) graduates.

19 Figures include UK and other EU-domiciled full-time, first-degree graduates from UK institutions, and were calculated from principal subject data provided by HESA from the Destinations of Leavers Survey and Student Record 2015/16. Proportions calculated based on the total of all graduates surveyed (including those in an unknown destination).

20 The report defines 'successful leaders as those who are in positions of influence within their organisation and their sectors more broadly'. British Council (2015). *The Educational Pathways of Leaders: An International Comparison*. London: British Council and Ipsos Public Affairs, p. 4.

21 Please note: In their report, the British Council separated what they defined as Social Studies (Anthropology, Communications, Economics, International Relations, Political Science, Psychology, and Law) from Business Fields (Business, Management, and Marketing) and Education (Education, English as a Second Language, and Pedagogy). For our purposes, we group all of these together for a total social sciences count and, as in the rest of this report, we consider Business & Management and Education to be part of the social sciences. See: British Council (2015). *The Educational Pathways of Leaders: An International Comparison*, p. 8.

22 This total figure for politicians breaks down to 57% from 'social sciences' graduates and 4% from 'business' graduates according to the breakdown in the British Council report terminology. See: British Council (2015). *The Educational Pathways of Leaders: An International Comparison*, p. 15.

23 This total figure for civil servants breaks down to 55% from 'social sciences' graduates and 7% from 'business' graduates according to the breakdown in the British Council report terminology. For financial services and consulting it is 42% social sciences and 28% business, and for law and legal services it is 89% social sciences and 4% business graduates. See: British Council (2015). *The Educational Pathways of Leaders: An International Comparison*, p. 15.

24 This total figure for energy and environment breaks down to 20% from 'social sciences' graduates and 30% from 'business' graduates according to the breakdown in the British Council report terminology. For technology and innovation it is 29% social sciences and 17% business, for health it is 22% social science and 18% business, and for defence and security it is 19% social sciences and 16% business graduates. See: British Council (2015). *The Educational Pathways of Leaders: An International Comparison*, p. 15.

25 Data sourced from Table 4 of the British Council report (2015). *The Educational Pathways of Leaders: An International Comparison*, p. 8.

26 British Council (2015). *The Educational Pathways of Leaders: An International Comparison*.

27 The median salary is the middle value between the highest and lowest salaries reported. We use the median salary rather than the mean salary, which represents the arithmetic average salary, because, as HESA notes, the mean 'could be skewed by a few abnormally high or low values. The median takes the middle value and is therefore less affected by very high or low salaries.' Source: HESA Destination of Leavers from Higher Education in the United Kingdom for the Academic Year 2015/16, Table 10.

28   Source: HESA Destination of Leavers from Higher Education in the United Kingdom for the Academic Year 2015/16, Table 10. Please note that figures are for UK-domiciled full-time first degree leavers of UK higher educations institutions only.

29   Figures include UK and other EU-domiciled full-time, first-degree graduates from UK institutions, and were calculated from principal subject data provided by HESA from the Destinations of Leavers Survey and Student Record 2015/16.

30   Britton, J., Dearden, L., Shepard, N. and Vignoles, A. (2016). *How English Domiciled Graduate Earnings Vary with Gender, Institution Attended, Subject, and Socioeconomic Background.* Institute for Fiscal Studies, IFS Working Paper W16/06, p. 26.

31   Britton, Dearden, Shepard and Vignoles (2016). *How English Domiciled Graduate Earnings Vary with Gender, Institution Attended, Subject, and Socioeconomic Background*, p. 26.

32   Britton, Dearden, Shepard and Vignoles (2016). *How English Domiciled Graduate Earnings Vary with Gender, Institution Attended, Subject, and Socioeconomic Background*, p. 39.

33   Britton, Dearden, Shepard and Vignoles (2016). *How English Domiciled Graduate Earnings Vary with Gender, Institution Attended, Subject, and Socioeconomic Background*, p. 39.

34   Data cover UK-domiciled first-degree graduates from English HEIs only for the graduating cohort 2003/04 and tax years 2005/06 to 2014/15. Self-assessment data are not included. Source: Longitudinal Education Outcomes (LEO) Dataset, Table 1c: Activity of graduates by subject and sex. Part of: Statistics on Higher Education Graduate Employment and Earnings, Higher Education Participation, and Data Collection and Statistical Returns. UK Department for Education, released: 4 August 2016. Available from: https://www.gov.uk/government/statistics/graduate-outcomes-longitudinal-education-outcomes-leo-data.

35   Data cover UK-domiciled first-degree graduates from English HEIs only for the graduating cohort 2003/04 and tax years 2005/06 to 2014/15. Earnings are reported in nominal figures (not adjusted for inflation), are rounded to the nearest £500 and have 'been weighted by full person equivalent (FPE)'. Earnings are also based on PAYE, and self-assessment data are not included, thus the data 'do not reflect employment outcomes for those who are self-employed'. For more information on how the data are reported, see: https://www.gov.uk/government/uploads/system/uploads/attachment_data/file/573831/SFR60_2016_LEO_main_text_v1.1.pdf. For the source of the data itself, see: Longitudinal Education Outcomes (LEO) Dataset, Table 1c: Activity of graduates by subject and sex. Part of: Statistics on Higher Education Graduate Employment and Earnings, Higher Education Participation, and Data Collection and Statistical Returns. UK Department for Education, released: 4 August 2016. Available from: https://www.gov.uk/government/statistics/graduate-outcomes-longitudinal-education-outcomes-leo-data.

36   Data cover UK-domiciled first-degree graduates from English HEIs only for the graduating cohort 2003/04 and tax years 2005/06 to 2014/15. Self-assessment data are not included. Source: Longitudinal Education Outcomes (LEO) Dataset, Table 1c: Activity of graduates by subject and sex. Part of: Statistics on Higher Education Graduate

Employment and Earnings, Higher Education Participation, and Data Collection and Statistical Returns. UK Department for Education, released: 4 August 2016. Available from: https://www.gov.uk/government/statistics/graduate-outcomes-longitudinal-education-outcomes-leo-data.

37 Measured impact of going to Russell Group universities is likely to arise partly because they are more selective in their entry requirements; partly because of the standard of education they offer; and partly because of their general reputation among employers.

38 The Russell Group universities are: the University of Birmingham, the University of Bristol, the University of Cambridge, Cardiff University, University of Durham, the University of Edinburgh, the University of Exeter, the University of Glasgow, Imperial College of Science, Technology and Medicine, King's College London, the University of Leeds, the University of Liverpool, London School of Economics and Political Science, the University of Manchester, University of Newcastle-upon-Tyne, University of Nottingham, the University of Oxford, Queen Mary University of London, the Queen's University of Belfast, the University of Sheffield, the University of Southampton, University College London, the University of Warwick and the University of York.

39 Figures include UK and other EU-domiciled full-time, first-degree graduates from UK institutions, and were calculated from principal subject data provided by HESA from the Destinations of Leavers Survey and Student Record 2015/16.

40 Britton et al. provide a deeper analysis of 17 of the 23 Russell Group universities, with some not being included either because they did not provide the needed permissions or because the sample of relevant students was too small to be relevant to the statistical analysis. See: Britton, Dearden, Shepard and Vignoles (2016). *How English Domiciled Graduate Earnings Vary with Gender, Institution Attended, Subject, and Socioeconomic Background*, p. 17.

41 Britton, Dearden, Shepard and Vignoles (2016). *How English Domiciled Graduate Earnings Vary with Gender, Institution Attended, Subject, and Socioeconomic Background*, pp. 31–36.

42 This is a reproduction of Figure 9 in Britton et al. (2016). As they highlight, it shows: 'Unconditional female 20th, 50th and 90th percentile earnings for the 1999 cohort in 2012/13 for HEPs ranked on their graduates' 2012/13 median earnings. There are 166 different institutions included, and one "other" institution which include several hundred institutions that issue only a handful of loans. Note: The log scale is not used here. Zeros are included.' Britton, Dearden, Shepard and Vignoles (2016). *How English Domiciled Graduate Earnings Vary with Gender, Institution Attended, Subject, and Socioeconomic Background*, p. 32.

43 This is a reproduction of Figure 11 in Britton et al. (2016). As they highlight, it shows: 'Unconditional male 20th, 50th and 90th percentile earnings for the 1999 cohort in 2012/13 for HEPs ranked on their graduates' 2012/13 median earnings. There are 168 different institutions included, and one "other" institution which include several

hundred institutions that issue only a handful of loans. Note: The log scale is not used here. Zeros are included.' Britton, Dearden, Shepard and Vignoles (2016). *How English Domiciled Graduate Earnings Vary with Gender, Institution Attended, Subject, and Socioeconomic Background*, p. 34.

44 Britton, Dearden, Shepard and Vignoles (2016). *How English Domiciled Graduate Earnings Vary with Gender, Institution Attended, Subject, and Socioeconomic Background*, p. 39.

45 Britton, Dearden, Shepard and Vignoles (2016). *How English Domiciled Graduate Earnings Vary with Gender, Institution Attended, Subject, and Socioeconomic Background*, p. 37.

46 British Academy (2017). *The Right Skills: Celebrating Skills in the Arts, Humanities, and Social Sciences*, pp. 9–11. Available from: https://www.britac.ac.uk/node/8554.

47 See Mason, Nathan and Rosso (2015). *State of the Nation: A Review of Evidence on the Supply and Demand of Quantitative Skills*.

48 See Mason, Nathan and Rosso (2015). *State of the Nation: A Review of Evidence on the Supply and Demand of Quantitative Skills*, p. 10.

49 CEBR (February 2016). *Report for SAS: The Value of Big Data and the Internet of Things to the UK Economy*, p. 6. Available at: https://www.sas.com/content/dam/SAS/en_gb/doc/analystreport/cebr-value-of-big-data.pdf.

50 CEBR (February 2016). *Report for SAS: The Value of Big Data and the Internet of Things to the UK Economy*, p. 6. Available at: https://www.sas.com/content/dam/SAS/en_gb/doc/analystreport/cebr-value-of-big-data.pdf.

51 Mason, Nathan and Rosso (2015). *State of the Nation: A Review of Evidence on the Supply and Demand of Quantitative Skills*.

52 See, for example, Campaign for Social Science (2017). *The Health of People: How the Social Sciences Can Improve Population Health*. Available at: https://campaignforsocialscience.org.uk/healthofpeople/.

53 See Hartley, S. (2017). *The Fuzzy and the Techie: Why the Liberal Arts Will Rule the Digital World*. New York: Houghton Mifflin Harcourt; and Kuchler, H. (2017); How Silicon Valley Learned to Love the Liberal Arts. *Financial Times*, November 1.

54 https://www.theguardian.com/media/2016/nov/17/fake-news-google-funding-fact-checking-us-election.

55 Hartley, S. (2017). *The Fuzzy and the Techie: Why the Liberal Arts Will Rule the Digital World*, p. 17.

56 Hartley, S. (2017). *The Fuzzy and the Techie: Why the Liberal Arts Will Rule the Digital World*, p. 12.

57 According to Mason *et al.*, there is a 'strong employer demand for QS [in the UK] (in conjunction with other skills), with several indicators that the currently available supply of QS may be insufficient to meet demand'. Mason, Nathan and Rosso (2015). *State of the Nation: A Review of Evidence on the Supply and Demand of Quantitative Skills*.

58 Mason, Nathan and Rosso (2015). *State of the Nation: A Review of Evidence on the Supply and Demand of Quantitative Skills*.

59   Mason, Nathan and Rosso (2015). State of the Nation: *A Review of Evidence on the Supply and Demand of Quantitative Skills.*

60   Data sourced from Table 3.2 'Highest level of quantitative skills used in jobs, 20–60 year olds, 1997, 2001, 2006 and 2012, population weighted', in Mason, Nathan and Rosso (2015). *State of the Nation: A Review of Evidence on the Supply and Demand of Quantitative Skills*, p. 30.

61   Mason, Nathan and Rosso (2015). *State of the Nation: A Review of Evidence on the Supply and Demand of Quantitative Skills.*

62   CBI (July 2017). *Helping the UK Thrive: CBI/Pearson Education and Skills Survey 2017.* London: Pearson, p. 8.

63   CBI (July 2017). *Helping the UK Thrive: CBI/Pearson Education and Skills Survey 2017*, p. 29.

64   CBI (July 2016). *The Right Combination: CBI/Pearson Education and Skills Survey 2016.* London: Pearson, p. 32.

65   According to Hodgen *et al.*, these categories may be defined as follows: 'High demand. Subjects for which a level 3 mathematics qualification, usually A or AS level, is in most cases essential. Subject Groups: Engineering and technology, Mathematical sciences, Physical sciences. Medium demand. Subjects which need mathematics, but where the demands are usually not as high as for the high demand subjects. In many cases the primary need is for statistics and the ability to analyse and interpret data. Subject Groups: Agriculture and related subjects, Architecture, building and planning, Biological sciences, Business and administrative studies, Computer science, Education, Medicine and dentistry, Social studies, Subjects allied to medicine, Veterinary science. Low demand. Subjects with generally low mathematical demands. Subject Groups: Combined/general subjects, Creative arts and design, Historical and philosophical studies, Languages, Law, Mass communications and documentation.' Hodgen, J., Adkins, M. and Tomei, A. (2017). *The Mathematical Backgrounds of Undergraduates: Interim Report.* Nottingham: University of Nottingham.

66   Table created using data and concepts from: Hodgen, Adkins and Tomei (2017). *The Mathematical Backgrounds of Undergraduates: Interim Report.* According to Hodgen *et al.*, these data cover the 'mathematical attainment for all honours students from the English GSCE cohort of 2007/2008, who completed A-level between 2008/2009 and 2010/2011' (pp. 4 & 5).

67   Data sourced from Table 8: Proportion of undergraduate intake with A level mathematics, by degree subject, in Hillman, J. (2014). *Mathematics after 16: The State of Play, Challenges, and Ways Ahead.* London: Nuffield Foundation, p. 22. Please note: Hillman's data are based on 2007 and 2010 UCAS data for UK-domiciled higher education applicants. Scotland is not covered by these data.

68   This graph uses new data to update a graph (Figure 2) originally created by Hillman in Hillman (2014). *Mathematics after 16: The State of Play, Challenges, and Ways Ahead*, p. 9. New data are sourced from https://www.jcq.org.uk/examination-results/a-levels/. Scotland is not covered by these data.

69   The 2017 Autumn Budget states that 'The government will … reward schools and colleges who support their students to study maths by giving them £600 for every extra pupil who decides to take Maths or Further Maths A levels or Core Maths – with over £80 million available initially, and no cap on numbers.' See Section 5.8, Autumn Budget 2017, HM Treasury. Available at: https://www.gov.uk/government/publications/autumn-budget-2017-documents/autumn-budget-2017.

70   Noyes, A. and Adkins, M. (2017). *Rethinking the Value of Advanced Mathematics Participation (REVAMP)*. Nottingham: University of Nottingham.

71   Although it should be noted that the actual increase in earnings an individual student might realise for an A level maths qualification on estimate 'varies between 2 and 21% of income[, …] dependent upon a range of other factors'. Noyes and Adkins (2017). *Rethinking the Value of Advanced Mathematics Participation (REVAMP)*.

72   Noyes and Adkins (2017). *Rethinking the Value of Advanced Mathematics Participation (REVAMP)*.

73   This is a reproduction of Figure 1 in Britton *et al.* (2016). As they highlight, it shows: 'Quantiles of female earnings for the 1999 cohort from three subjects compared to the quantiles for all female graduates. No control variables are used for intake. Discrete points are taken from the distribution, at the 10th, 20th… 90th, 95th quantiles, with linear interpolation in between. This may give the impression of understating the share with zero earnings, for example. Scatter points to the right of each Figure show the corresponding mean for each case (the horizontal positioning of the dots is entirely random, this added jitter makes the dots easier to read). Note earnings are displayed on a log scale.' Britton, Dearden, Shepard and Vignoles (2016). *How English Domiciled Graduate Earnings Vary with Gender, Institution Attended, Subject, and Socioeconomic Background*, p. 22.

74   This is a reproduction of Figure 2 in Britton *et al.* (2016). As they highlight, it shows: 'Quantiles of male earnings for the 1999 cohort for three subjects compared to the quantiles for all male graduates. No control variables are used for intake. Discrete points are taken from the distribution, at the 10th, 20th… 90th, 95th quantiles, with linear interpolation in between. This may give the impression of understating the share with zero earnings, for example. Scatter points to the right of each Figure show the corresponding mean for each case (the horizontal positioning of the dots is entirely random, this added jitter makes the dots easier to read). Note earnings are displayed on a log scale.' Britton, Dearden, Shepard and Vignoles (2016). *How English Domiciled Graduate Earnings Vary with Gender, Institution Attended, Subject, and Socioeconomic Background*, p. 24.

75   Noyes and Adkins (2017). *Rethinking the Value of Advanced Mathematics Participation (REVAMP)*.

76   Noyes and Adkins (2017). *Rethinking the Value of Advanced Mathematics Participation (REVAMP)*.

77   Adkins, M. and Noyes, A. (2016). Reassessing the economic value of advanced level mathematics. *British Education Journal*, 42 (1): 93–116.

78   The groupings of subjects by level of quantitative skill is borrowed from Hodgen, Adkins and Tomei (2017). *The Mathematical Backgrounds of Undergraduates: Interim Report.*

79   Source: HESA Table 6a – Destinations of full-time first-degree leavers by sex, activity and subject area 2011/12 to 2015/16.

80   Sloane, P. and O'Leary, J. (June 2004). The Return to a University Education in Great Britain. IZA DP No. 1199, Discussion Paper Series. IZA – Forschungsinstitut zur Zukunft der Arbeit (Institute for the Study of Labour).

81   Data for tables sourced from Tables 6 and 7 in Sloane and O'Leary (June 2004). The Return to a University Education in Great Britain. IZA DP No. 1199, Discussion Paper Series. IZA – Forschungsinstitut zur Zukunft der Arbeit (Institute for the Study of Labour).

82   See, for example, some of the many studies cited in Selingo, Jeffrey (2017). Six Myths about Choosing a College Major, *The New York Times*, November 3. Available at: https://www.nytimes.com/2017/11/03/education/edlife/choosing-a-college-major.html?hpw&rref=education&action=click&pgtype=Homepage&module=well-region&region=bottom-well&WT.nav=bottom-well&_r=0

83   Per note 67 above, see Section 5.8, Autumn Budget 2017, HM Treasury. Available at: https://www.gov.uk/government/publications/autumn-budget-2017-documents/autumn-budget-2017.

84   Nuffield Foundation (2012). *Mathematics in A Level Assessments: A Report on the Mathematical Content of A Level Assessments in Business Studies, Computing, Economics, Geography, Psychology and Sociology.* London: Nuffield Foundation.

85   *Smith Review of Post-16 Mathematics* (20 July 2017). Available at: https://www.gov.uk/government/publications/smith-review-of-post-16-maths-report-and-government-response.

86   Source: HESA Destination of Leavers from Higher Education in the United Kingdom for the Academic Year 2015/16, Table 10.

87   Figures include UK and other EU-domiciled full-time, first-degree graduates from UK institutions, and were calculated from principal subject data provided by HESA from the Destinations of Leavers Survey and Student Record 2015/16. Data for psychology (C8) graduates included.

88   Please note, these data cover UK-domiciled first-degree graduates from English HEIs only for the graduating cohort 2003/04 and tax years 2005/06 to 2014/15. Self-assessment data are not included. Source: Longitudinal Education Outcomes (LEO) Dataset, Table 1c: Activity of graduates by subject and sex. Part of: Statistics on Higher Education Graduate Employment and Earnings, Higher Education Participation, and Data Collection and Statistical Returns. UK Department for Education, released: 4 August 2016. Available from: https://www.gov.uk/government/statistics/graduate-outcomes-longitudinal-education-outcomes-leo-data.